WORDS
OF
WISDOM

A Book of Inspiration

WORDS
OF
WISDOM

A Book of Inspiration

Ariel Books
Andrews and McMeel
Kansas City

10 9 8 7 6 5 4

ISBN: 0-8362-3003-5

Library of Congress Catalog
Card Number: 91-77105

Design: Michael Mendelsohn

INTRODUCTION

Wisdom means something different to each of us, yet there is a golden thread that unites the words of great thinkers and writers—a common instinct for truth.

Collected here is a sampling of the sages—reflections and advice on life's joys, beauties, lessons, and eternal truths. The quotations are drawn from a diversity of writers and thinkers, but their messages echo one another: Find joy in simplicity, take heart, seize the day, be open to mystery, and believe in the many miracles around you.

To every thing there is a season, and a time to every purpose under the heaven.

Ecclesiastes 3:1

The true way goes over a rope which is not stretched at any great height but just above the ground. It seems more designed to make men stumble than to be walked upon.

FRANZ KAFKA

Ride the horse in the direction that it's going.

WERNER ERHARD

Live not as though there were a thousand years ahead of you. Fate is at your elbow; make yourself good while life and power are still yours.

MARCUS AURELIUS

Follow your bliss.

JOSEPH CAMPBELL

A living dog is better than a dead lion.

Ecclesiastes 9:4

You should treat all disasters as if they were trivialities but never treat a triviality as if it were a disaster.

QUENTIN CRISP

No man can serve two masters: for either he will hate the one, and love the other; or else he will hold to the one, and despise the other. Ye cannot serve God and mammon.

Matthew 6:24

Take therefore no thought for the morrow: for the morrow shall take thought for the things of itself. Sufficient unto the day is the evil thereof.

Matthew 6:34

All of life is six to five against.

DAMON RUNYON

There is in man an upwelling spring of life, energy, love, whatever you like to call it. If a course is not cut for it, it turns the ground round it into a swamp.

MARK RUTHERFORD

A man who has faith must be prepared not only to be a martyr, but to be a fool.

G. K. CHESTERTON

The purpose of life is a life of purpose.

ROBERT BYRNE

The happiest people seem to be those who have no particular reason for being happy except that they are so.

W. R. INGE

Growth is a greater mystery than death. All of us can understand failure, we all contain failure and death within us, but not even the successful man can begin to describe the impalpable elations and apprehensions of growth.

NORMAN MAILER

Happiness is a how, not a what; a talent, not an object.

HERMANN HESSE

The man who has lived the longest is not he who has spent the greatest number of years, but he who has had the greatest sensibility of life.

JEAN-JACQUES ROUSSEAU

If you do not hope, you will not find what is beyond your hopes.

ST. CLEMENT OF ALEXANDRIA

The natural flights of the human mind are not from pleasure to pleasure but from hope to hope.

DR. JOHNSON

To be angry is to revenge the faults of others upon ourselves.

ALEXANDER POPE

An ill-humoured man is a prisoner at the mercy of an enemy from whom he can never escape.

SA'DI

It is not easy to find happiness in ourselves, and it is impossible to find it elsewhere.

AGNES REPPLIER

No one can make you feel inferior without your consent.

ELEANOR ROOSEVELT

If we only wanted to be happy, it would be easy; but we want to be happier than other people, and that is almost always difficult, since we think them happier than they are.

MONTESQUIEU

He hath scattered the proud in the imagination
   of their hearts.
He hath put down the mighty from their seats,
   and exalted them of low degree.

Luke 1:51-52

We spend our time envying people whom we
wouldn't wish to be.

JEAN ROSTAND

We are no more responsible for the evil thoughts which pass through our minds, than a scarecrow for the birds which fly over the seed-plot he has to guard; the sole responsibility in each case is to prevent them from settling.

CHURTON COLLINS

Temptation laughs at the fool who takes it seriously.

THE CHOFETZ CHAIM

A fool's paradise is a wise man's hell.

THOMAS FULLER

Waste no more time arguing what a good man should be. Be one.

MARCUS AURELIUS

If there is any peace it will come through being, not knowing.

HENRY MILLER

The best way to avoid a bad action is by doing a good one, for there is no difficulty in the world like that of trying to do nothing.

JOHN CLARE

Stupidity consists in wanting to reach conclusions. We are a thread, and we want to know the whole cloth.

GUSTAVE FLAUBERT

There are some people that if they don't know, you can't tell 'em.

LOUIS ARMSTRONG

❖ 30 ❖

A man should never be ashamed to own that he has been in the wrong, which is but saying, in other words, that he is wiser today than he was yesterday.

JONATHAN SWIFT

Be happy. It is a way of being wise.

COLETTE

Of cheerfulness, or a good temper — the more it is spent, the more of it remains.

RALPH WALDO EMERSON

There's an element of truth in every idea that lasts long enough to be called corny.

IRVING BERLIN

Wisdom is ofttimes nearer when we stoop than when we soar.

WILLIAM WORDSWORTH

Goodness is uneventful. It does not flash, it glows.

DAVID GRAYSON

Human felicity is produced not so much by great pieces of good fortune that seldom happen, as by little advantages that occur every day.

BENJAMIN FRANKLIN

Perhaps the most despairing cry of the pessimistic mind is that the world is never quite as bad as it ought and should be for intellectual purposes.

BERNARD BERENSON

When the moon is not full, the stars shine more brightly.

BUGANDA PROVERB

He that wrestles with us strengthens our nerves, and sharpens our skill. Our antagonist is our helper.

EDMUND BURKE

The thing we run from we run to.

ROBERT ANTHONY

If we are not our brother's keeper, let us at least not be his executioner.

MARLON BRANDO

The wicked are always surprised to find that the good can be clever.

MARQUIS DE VAUVENARGUES

God is ashamed when the prosperous boast of his special favour.

RABINDRANATH TAGORE

We all may have come on different ships, but we're in the same boat now.

MARTIN LUTHER KING, JR.

If some persons died, and others did not die,
death would indeed be a terrible affliction.

LA BRUYÈRE

While I thought that I was learning how to live,
I have been learning how to die.

LEONARDO DA VINCI

Give sorrow words. The grief that does not
   speak
Whispers the o'erfraught heart and bids it
   break.

WILLIAM SHAKESPEARE

Better a tooth out than always aching.

THOMAS FULLER

It has been my experience that people who have no vices have very few virtues.

ABRAHAM LINCOLN

FATHER OF LIGHT

Father of light, to Thee I call;
My soul is dark within.
Thou who canst mark the sparrow's fall,
Avert the death of sin.
Thou who canst guide the wandering star,

A Book of Inspiration

Who calm'st the elemental war,
Whose mantle is yon boundless sky;
My thoughts, my words, my crimes forgive,
And, since I soon must cease to live,
Instruct me how to die.

GEORGE GORDON, LORD BYRON

Cowardice, as distinguished from panic, is almost always simply a lack of ability to suspend the functioning of the imagination.

ERNEST HEMINGWAY

If you're going to tell people the truth, be funny or they'll kill you.

BILLY WILDER

Words of Wisdom

Good things, when short, are twice as good.

BALTASAR GRACIA'N

It's either easy or impossible.

SALVADOR DALI

The art of being wise is the art of knowing what to overlook.

WILLIAM JAMES

Life is short; live it up.

NIKITA KHRUSHCHEV

Experience is not what happens to a man, it's what a man does with what happens to him.

ALDOUS HUXLEY

Happiness is not something you experience, it's something you remember.

OSCAR LEVANT

Life is a great bundle of little things.

OLIVER WENDELL HOLMES

A trifle consoles us because a trifle upsets us.

BLAISE PASCAL

It is very dangerous to go into eternity with possibilities which one has oneself prevented from becoming realities. A possibility is a hint from God.

SØREN KIERKEGAARD

No matter what you do, do your best at it. If you're going to be a bum, be the best bum there is.

ROBERT MITCHUM

Our remedies oft in ourselves do lie,
Which we ascribe to heaven.

WILLIAM SHAKESPEARE

Life is what happens when you are making other plans.

JOHN LENNON

Almost every man wastes part of his life in attempts to display qualities which he does not possess, and to gain applause which he cannot keep.

DR. JOHNSON

Are we to look at cherry blossoms only in full bloom, the moon only when it is cloudless? To long for the moon while looking on the rain, to lower the blinds and be unaware of the passing of the spring—these are even more deeply moving. Branches about to blossom or gardens strewn with flowers are worthier of our admiration.

YOSHIDA KENKO

All passions exaggerate: it is only because they exaggerate that they are passions.

CHAMFORT

Whoever is abandoned by hope has also been abandoned by fear; this is the meaning of the word "desperate."

ARTHUR SCHOPENHAUER

Hurry? I have no time to hurry.

IGOR STRAVINSKY

A stumble may prevent a fall.

THOMAS FULLER

Man is so made that he can only find relaxation
from one kind of labour by taking up another.

ANATOLE FRANCE

Many a man would rather you heard his story
than granted his request.

LORD CHESTERFIELD

When you meet someone better than yourself, turn your thoughts to becoming his equal. When you meet someone not as good as you are, look within and examine your own self.

CONFUCIUS

All things whatsoever ye would that men should do to you, do ye even so to them: for this is the law of the prophets.

Matthew 7:12

The old law about "an eye for an eye" leaves everybody blind.

MARTIN LUTHER KING, JR.

Evil is uncertain in the same degree as good, and for the reason that we ought not to hope too securely, we ought not to fear with too much dejection.

DR. JOHNSON

I have a simple philosophy. Fill what's empty. Empty what's full. Scratch where it itches.

ALICE ROOSEVELT LONGWORTH

Humor is the shortest distance between two people.

VICTOR BORGE

 68 ✣

When I'm working on a problem, I never think about beauty. I think only of how to solve the problem; but when I'm finished, if the solution is not beautiful, I know it is wrong.

R. BUCKMINSTER FULLER

Self-satire, disillusion, absence of prejudice may
be freedom, but they are not strength.

HENRI FRÉDÉRIC AMIEL

A man with one watch knows what time it is.
A man with two watches is never sure.

JOHN PEER

No matter how cynical you become, it's never enough to keep up.

JANE WAGNER

Blessed is he who expects nothing, for he shall never be disappointed.

ALEXANDER POPE

Pleasure is very seldom found where it is sought; our brightest blazes of gladness are commonly kindled by unexpected sparks.

DR. JOHNSON

I do not admire the excess of a virtue like courage unless I see at the same time an excess of the opposite virtue, as in Epaminondas, who possessed extreme courage and extreme kindness. We show greatness not by being at one extreme, but by touching both at once and occupying all the space in between.

PASCAL

There's right and there's wrong. You get to do one or the other. You do the one, and you're living. You do the other, and you may be walking around but you're dead as a beaver hat.

JOHN WAYNE

A man cannot become an atheist merely by wishing it.

NAPOLEON BONAPARTE

The only Zen you find on the top of mountains is the Zen you bring there.

ROBERT PIRSIG

❖ 76 ❖

The fool doth think he is wise, but the wise man knows himself to be a fool.

WILLIAM SHAKESPEARE

Wise men talk because they have something to say; fools talk because they have to say something.

PLATO

Manifest plainness,
Embrace simplicity,
Reduce selfishness,
Have few desires.

LAO-TZU

Computers are useless. They can only give you answers.

PABLO PICASSO

Talk low, talk slow, and don't say too much.

JOHN WAYNE

Some things have to be believed to be seen.

RALPH HODGSON

The text face for this book was designed by Jan Tschichold.

The sources for the design are to be found on a specimen sheet of the Frankfurt typefounder, Conrad Berner, who married the widow of another typefounder, Jacques Sabon—hence the name of the face. The roman is based on a font engraved by Garamond and the italic on a font by Granjon, but Tschichold has introduced many refinements to make these models suitable for the typographic needs of today.

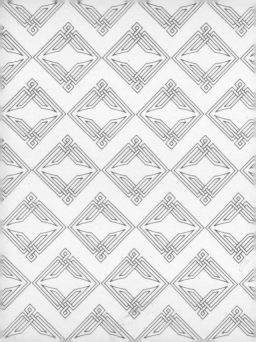